*Songs to Joannes &*
# OTHER
V E R S E

*BY*

*Mina Loy*

# FORGOTTEN POETS

Editor | Dick Whyte                                    Number 7 | 2022

**MINA LOY (1882-1966)** was born in London to wealthy parents. While her father did not believe in formal education for women, Loy convinced him to let her study at Künstlerinnenverein, a women's arts college in Munich, and the Académie Colarossi, in Paris. She became close with Gertrude Stein while living in France, and then moved to Florence in 1906. Loy began publishing 'free verse' in 1914, dabbled in Futurism, and then in 1916 moved to New York to join the avant-garde art and literary scene, alongside Dadaists like Marcel Duchamp, Man Ray, Francis Picabia, and publishers Jane Heap and Margaret Anderson (et al.). Loy would go on to become a leading poet of the post-1913 'new verse' movement—culminating in her 1923 book, *Lunar Baedeker*—and her poetic innovations were praised by numerous contemporaries, including William Carlos Williams, Alfred Kreymborg, Walter Arensberg, and T.S. Elliot. Though it would be 25 years until Loy would publish a second book of poetry, she continued to write and make assemblages until her death in 1966.

Publication credits: 'Songs to Joannes' (*Others*, April 1917); 'I-IV' first published as 'Love Songs' (July 1915); 'There Is No Life Or Death' (*Camera Work*, 1914); 'Parturition' (*The Trend*, Oct. 1914); 'Sketch of a Man' (*Rogue*, April 1915); 'Virgin Plus Curtains' (Aug. 1915); 'Babies in Hospital' (1916); 'At the Door of the House' & 'Human Cylinders' (*Others*, 1917); 'The Dead' (1919); 'O Hell' (*Contact*, Dec. 1920); 'Poe' (*The Dial*, Oct. 1922); 'Mexican Desert' (June 1922); 'Perlun' (Aug. 1921); 'Brancusi's Golden Bird' (Nov. 1922); 'Apology of Genius' [Harriet Monroe's edit] (*Poetry*, Nov. 1923); many of these, along with 'Ignoramus' (ca. 1915), 'Joyce's Ulysses', & '"The Starry Sky" of Wyndham Lewis' (etc.) also appeared in Loy's first book, *Lunar Baedeker* (1923); 'Marble' & 'Gertrude Stein' (*Transatlantic Review*, 1923-4). 'Other Words': 'Aphorisms on Futurism' (*Camera Work*, Jan. 1914); 'Free Verse' & 'In... Formation' (*The Blind Man*, May 1917); 'Psycho-Democracy' (*The Little Review*, Autumn 1921).

Cover: R.A. Wilson – 'A Design' (*The Apple*, April 1920) & Philip Hadgreen – 'Wood-cut' (*The Chapbook*, Jan. 1923); Inside: Mina Loy – 'Baby's Head' (*The Dial*, Feb. 1922); 'Portrait I' & 'Portrait II' (April 1921); Clara Tice – 'Edgar Varèse' (*The Blind Man*, May 1917), assorted drawings (*Bruno's Weekly & Greenwich Village*, 1915-16), & 'Who's Who in Manhattan' (*Cartoons Magazine*, Aug. 1917); with Wyndham Lewis – 'A Prayer' (*The Chapbook*, 1925); Djuna Barnes & Mina Loy - 'Two Portraits of James Joyce' (*Vanity Fair*, 1922), etc.

**FORGOTTEN PRESS**
Aotearoa | New Zealand

ISBN: 978-1-991310-35-4 (paperback) • 978-1-991310-36-1 (hardback)
978-1-991310-37-8 (ebook)

# MINA LOY

## SONGS TO JOANNES & OTHER VERSE

━━  ━━  ━━  ━━  ━━

## SONGS TO JOANNES

The complete 42 song-cycle, originally
published in *Others* (1915-17).

## OTHER SONGS

A selection of verses from *Lunar Baedecker* (1923),
& various magazines & journals.

## OTHER WORDS

A selection of short essays from the Dada magazine
*The Blind Man* (1917).

━━  ━━  ━━  ━━  ━━

# FORGOTTEN POETS

*edited by* **Dick Whyte**.

### *Missing Meters! Lost Lyrics! Vanished Verses!*

LEWIS ALEXANDER
PEARL ANDELSON
IRIS BARRY
GWENDOLYN BENNETT
ADELAIDE CRAPSEY
MARY CAROLYN DAVIES
HILDA DOOLITTLE
HILDEGARDE FLANNER
F.S. FLINT
JUN FUJITA
SADAKICHI HARTMANN
T.E. HULME
TAKEKO KUJO
AMY LOWELL
MINA LOY
YONE NOGUCHI
CHARLES REZNIKOFF
EDWARD STORER
MARIE TUDOR-GARLAND
AKIKO YOSHINO
AKIKO YANAGIWARA
& MANY MORE

FORGOTTENPOETS.COM

# Songs to Joannes

## APRIL, 1917

I

Spawn   of   Fantasies
Silting the appraisable
Pig Cupid   his rosy snout
Rooting erotic garbage
"Once upon a time"
Pulls a weed   white and star-topped
Among wild oats   sewn in mucous-membrane

I would    an    eye in a bengal light
Eternity in a sky-rocket
Constellations in an ocean
Whose rivers run no fresher
Than a trickle of saliva

These    are suspect places

I must live in my lantern
Trimming subliminal flicker
Virginal    to the bellows
Of Experience
                    Coloured glass

## II

        The skin-sack
In which a wanton duality
Packed
All the completions of my infructuous impulses
Something the shape of a man
To the casual vulgarity of the merely observant
More of a clock-work mechanism
Running down against time
To which I am not paced
  My finger-tips are numb from fretting
    your hair
A God's door-mat

       On the threshold of your mind

## III

We might have coupled
In the bed-ridden monopoly of a moment
Or broken flesh with one another
At the profane communion table
Where wine is spill't on promiscuous lips

We might have given birth to a butterfly
With the daily-news
Printed in blood on its wings

## IV

Once in a mezzanino
The starry ceiling
Vaulted an unimaginable family
Bird-like abortions
With human throats
And Wisdom's eyes
Who wore lamp-shade red dresses
And woolen hair

One bore a baby
In a padded porte-enfant
Tied with a sarsenet ribbon
To her goose's wings




But for the abominable shadows
I would have lived
Among their fearful furniture
To teach them to tell me their secrets
Before I guessed
—Sweeping the brood clean out

## V

    Midnight empties the street
Of all but us
Three
I am undecided which way back
           To the left a boy
—One wing has been washed in the rain
  The other will never be clean any more—
Pulling door-bells to remind
Those that are snug
          To the right a haloed ascetic
          Threading houses
Probes wounds for souls
—The poor can't wash in hot water—
And I don't know which turning to take
Since you got home to yourself—first

## VI

I know the Wire-Puller intimately
And if it were not for the people
On whom you keep one eye
You could look straight at me
And Time would be set back

## VII

My pair of feet
Smack the flag-stones
That are something left over from your walking
The wind stuffs the scum of the white street
Into my lungs and my nostrils
Exhilarated birds
Prolonging flight into the night
Never reaching — — — — — — —

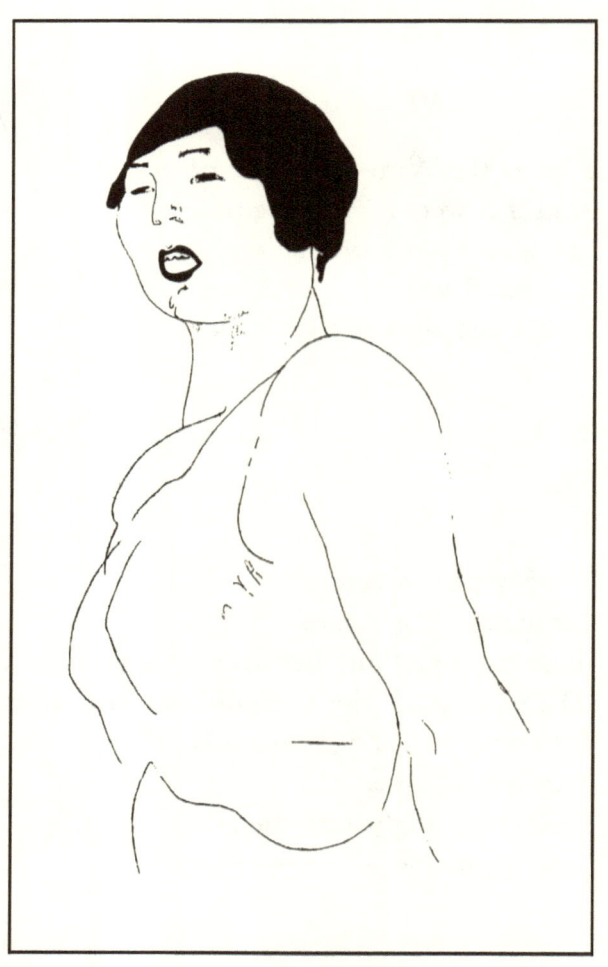

## VIII

I am the jealous store-house of the candle-ends
That lit your adolescent learning

— — — — — — — — — — — —

Behind God's eyes
There might
Be other lights

## IX

When we lifted
Our eye-lids on Love
A cosmos
Of coloured voices
And laughing honey

And spermatozoa
At the core of Nothing
In the milk of the Moon

## X

Shuttle-cock and battle-door
A little pink-love
And feathers are strewn

## XI

Dear one   at your mercy
Our Universe
Is only
A colorless onion
You derobe
Sheath by sheath
                    Remaining
A disheartening odour
About your nervy hands

## XII

Voices break on the confines of passion
Desire   Suspicion  Man   Woman
Solve in the humid carnage

Flesh from flesh
Draws the inseparable delight
Kissing at gasps   to catch it

Is it true
That I have set you apart
Inviolate in an utter crystallization
Of all   the jolting of the crowd
Taught me willingly to live to share

Or are you
Only the other half
Of an ego's necessity
Scourging pride with compassion
To the shallow sound of dissonance
And boom of escaping breath

## XIII

Come to me     There is something
I have got to tell you    and I can't tell
Something taking shape
Something that has a new name
A new dimension
A new use
A new illusion

It is ambient          And it is in your eyes
Something shiny     Something only for you
                        Something that I must not see

It is in my ears        Something very resonant
Something that you must not hear
                        Something only for me

Let us be very jealous
Very suspicious
Very conservative
Very cruel
Or we might make an end of the jostling
   of aspirations
Disorb inviolate egos

Where two or three are welded together
They shall become god

— — — — — — — — —

Oh that's right
Keep away from me  Please give me a push
Don't let me understand you  Don't realise me
Or we might tumble together
Depersonalized
Identical
Into the terrific Nirvana
Me you—you—me

## XIV

Today
Everlasting   passing   apparent   imperceptible
      To you
      I bring the nascent virginity of
      —Myself for the moment

      No love or the other thing
      Only the impact of lighted bodies
      Knocking sparks off each other
      In chaos

## XV

Seldom   Trying for Love
Fantasy dealt them out as gods
Two or three men   looked only human
But you alone
Superhuman   apparently
I had to be caught in the weak eddy
Of your drivelling humanity
                         To love you most


## XVI

We might have lived together
In the lights of the Arno
Or gone apple stealing under the sea
Or played
Hide and seek in love and cob-webs
And a lullaby on a tin-pan

And   talked till there were no more tongues
To talk with
And never have known any better

## XVII

I don't care
Where the legs of the legs of the furnature
    are walking to
Or what is hidden in the shadows they stride
Or what would look at me
If the shutters were not shut

Red   a warm colour on the battle-field
Heavy on my knees as a counterpane
Count counter
I counted   the fringe of the towel
Till two tassels clinging together
Let the square room fall away
From a round vacuum
Dilating with my breath

## XVIII

Out of the severing
Of hill from hill
The interim
Of star from star
The nascent
Static
Of night

## XIX

Nothing so conserving
As cool cleaving
Note of the Q H U
Clear carving
Breath-giving
Pollen smelling
Space

White telling
Of slaking
Drinkable
Through fingers
Running water
Grass haulms
Grow to

Leading astray
Of fireflies
Aerial quadrille
Bouncing
Off one another
Again conjoining
In recaptured pulses
Of light

You too
Had something
At that time
Of a green-lit glow-worm

— — — — — — — —

Yet slowly drenched
To raylessness
In rain

## XX

Let Joy go solace-winged
To flutter whom she may concern

## XXI

I store up nights against you
Heavy with shut-flower's nightmares

————————————

Stack noons
Curled to the solitaire
Core of the
Sun

## XXII

Green things grow
Salads
For the cerebral
Forager's revival
Upon bossed bellies
Of mountains
Rolling in the sun
And flowered flummery
Breaks
To my silly shoes

In ways without you
I go
Gracelessly
As things go

## XXIII

Laughter in solution
Stars in a stare
Irredeemable pledges
Of pubescent consummations
Rot
To the recurrent moon
Bleach
To the pure white
Wickedness of pain

## XXIV

The procreative truth of Me
Petered out
In pestilent
Tear drops
Little lusts and lucidities
And prayerful lies
Muddled with the heinous acerbity
Of your street-corner smile

## XXV

Licking the Arno
The little rosy
Tongue of Dawn
Interferes with our eyelashes

— — — — — — — — —

We twiddle to it
Round and round
Faster
And turn into machines

Till the sun
Subsides in shining
Melts some of us
Into abysmal pigeon-holes
Passion has bored
In warmth

Some few of us
Grow to the level of cool plains
Cutting our foot-hold
With steel eyes

## XXVI

Shedding our petty pruderies
From slit eyes
We sidle up
To Nature
— — — that irate pornographist

## XXVII

    Nucleus    Nothing
Inconceivable concept
Insentient repose
The hands of races
Drop off from
Immodifiable plastic

The contents
Of our ephemeral conjunction
In aloofness from Much
Flowed to approachment of — — — —
NOTHING
There was a man and a woman
In the way
While the Irresolvable
Rubbed with our daily deaths
Impossible eyes

## XXVIII

The steps go up for ever
And they are white
And the first step   is the last white
Forever
Coloured   conclusions
Smelt   to synthetic
Whiteness
Of my
Emergence
And I am burnt quite white
In the climacteric
Withdrawal of your sun
And wills and words all white
Suffuse
Illimitable monotone

White  where there is nothing to see
But a white towel
Wipes the cymophanous sweat
—Mist rise of living—
From your
Etiolate body
And the white dawn
Of your   New Day
Shuts down on me


Unthinkable   that white over there
— — — Is smoke from your house

## XXIX

Evolution fall foul of
Sexual equality
Prettily miscalculate
Similitude

Unnatural selection
Breed such sons and daughters
As shall jibber at each other
Uninterpretable cryptonyms
Under the moon

Give them some way of
    braying brassily
For caressive calling
Or to homophonous hiccoughs
Transpose the laugh
Let them suppose that tears
Are snowdrops or molasses
Or anything
Than human insufficiencies
Begging dorsal vertebrae

Let meeting be the turning
To the antipodean
And Form a blurr
Anything
Than seduce them
To the one
As simple satisfaction
For the other

Let them clash together
From their incognitoes
In seismic orgasm

For far further
Differentiation
Rather than watch
Own-self distortion
Wince in the alien ego

## XXX

In some
Prenatal plagiarism
Foetal buffoons
Caught tricks

— — — — —

From archetypal pantomime
Stringing emotions
Looped aloft

— — — —

For the blind eyes
That Nature knows us with
And the most of Nature is green

— — — — — — — — — —

What guaranty
For the proto-form
We fumble
Our souvenir ethics to

— — — — — — — —

## XXXI

Crucifixion
Of a busy-body
Longing to interfere so
With the intimacies
Of your insolent isolation

Crucifixion
Of an illegal ego's
Eclosion
On your equilibrium
Caryatid of an idea

Crucifixion
Wracked arms
Index extremities
In vacuum
To the unbroken fall

## XXXII

The moon is cold
Joannes
Where the Mediterranean— — — — —

## XXXIII

The prig of passion— — — —
To your professorial paucity

Proto-plasm was raving mad
Evolving us— — —

## XXXIV

Love — — — the preeminent literateur

# OTHER *Songs*

**1914–1924.**

There is no Life or Death,
Only activity
And in the absolute
Is no declivity.
There is no Love or Lust
Only propensity
Who would possess
Is a nonentity.
There is no First or Last
Only equality
And who would rule
Joins the majority.
There is no Space or Time
Only intensity,
And tame things
    Have no immensity.

# P a r t u r i t i o n

I am the centre
Of a circle of pain
Exceeding its boundaries in every direction

The business of the bland sun
Has no affair with me
In my congested cosmos of agony
From which there is no escape
On infinitely prolonged nerve-vibrations
Or in contraction
To the pinpoint nucleus of being
Locate an irritation     without
It is                         within
Within
It is without.
The sensitized area
Is identical     with the extensity
Of intension

I am the false quantity
In the harmony of physiological
potentiality
To which
Gaining self-control
I should be consonant
In time

Pain is no stronger than the resisting force
Pain calls up in me
The struggle is equal

The open window is full of a voice
A fashionable portrait painter
Running upstairs to a woman's apartment
Sings
       "All the girls are tid'ly did'ly
       All the girls are nice
       Whether they wear their hair in curls
       Or—"


At the back of the thoughts
   to which I permit crystallization
      The conception          Brute
      Why?
         The irresponsibility of the male
      Leaves woman her superior Inferiority

He is running upstairs
I am climbing a distorted mountain of agony
Incidentally with the exhaustion of control
I reach the summit
And gradually subside into anticipation of
Repose
Which never comes.

For another mountain is growing up
Which       goaded by the unavoidable
I must traverse
Traversing myself

Something in the delirium of night hours
Confuses while intensifying sensibility
Blurring spatial contours
So aiding elusion of the circumscribed
That the gurgling of a crucified wild beast
Comes from so far away
And the foam on the stretched muscles
    of a mouth
Is no part of myself
There is a climax in sensibility
When pain surpassing itself
Becomes exotic
And the ego succeeds in unifying the positive
    and negative poles of sensation
Uniting the opposing and resisting forces
In lascivious revelation

Relaxation
Negation of myself as a unit
Vacuum interlude
I should have been emptied of life
Giving life
For consciousness in crises        races
Through the subliminal deposits
    of evolutionary processes




Have I    not
Somewhere
Scrutinized
A dead white feathered moth
Laying eggs?

A moment
Being realization
Can
Vitalized by cosmic initiation
Furnish an adequate apology
For the objective
Agglomeration of activities
Of a life
LIFE

A leap with nature
Into the essence
Of unpredicted Maternity
Against my thigh
Tough of infinitesimal motion
Scarcely perceptible
Undulation
Warmth          moisture
  Stir of incipient life
Precipitating into me
The contents of the universe

Mother I am
Identical
With infinite Maternity
    Indivisible
    Acutely
    I am absorbed
    Into
The was—is—ever—shall—be
Of cosmic reproductivity

Rises from the subconscious
Impression of a cat
With blind kittens
Among her legs
Same undulating life-stir
I am that cat

Rises from the subconscious
Impression of small animal carcass
Covered with blue bottles
—Epicurean—

And through the insects
Waves that same undulation of living
Death
Life
I am knowing
All about

      Unfolding




The next morning
Each woman-of-the-people
Tiptoeing the red pile of the carpet
Doing hushed service

Each woman-of-the-people
Wearing a halo
A ludicrous little halo
Of which she is sublimely    unaware

I once heard in a church
—Man and woman God made them—
Thank God.

## Sketch Of A
## Man On A Platform

Man of absolute physical equilibrium
You stand so straight on your legs
Every plank or clod you plant your feet on
Becomes roots for those limbs

Among the men you accrete to yourself
You are more heavy
And more light
Force being most equitably disposed
Is easiest to lift from the ground
So at the same time
Your movements
Unassailable
Savor of the airy-fairy of the ballet
The essence of a Mademoiselle Genée
Winks in the to-and-fro of your cuff-links

Your projectile nose
Has meddled in the more serious business
Of the battle-field
With the same incautious aloofness
Of intense occupation
That it snuffles the trail of the female
And the comfortable
Passing odors of love

Your genius
So much less in your brain
Than in your body
Reinforcing the hitherto negligible
Qualities
Of life
Deals so exclusively with
The vital
That it is equally happy expressing itself
Through the activity of pushing
THINGS
In the opposite direction
To that which they are lethargically
     willing to go
As in the amative language
Of the eyes

Fundamentally unreliable
You leave others their initial strength
Concentrating
On stretching the theoretic elastic
    of your conceptions
Till the extent is adequate
To the hooking on
Of any—or all
Forms of creative idiosyncrasy
While the occasional snap
Of actual production
Stings the face of the public.

# Virgin Plus
# Curtains Minus Dots

Houses hold virgins
The doors on the chain

'Plumb streets with hearts'
'Bore curtains with eyes'

Virgins      without dots
Stare        beyond probability

See the men pass
Their hats are not ours
We          take a walk
They are going somewhere
And they    may look everywhere
Men's eyes   look into things
Our eyes      look out

A great deal of ourselves
We offer to the mirror
Something less to the confessional
The rest      to Time
There is so much      Time
Everything is full of it
                    Such a long time


Virgins may whisper
'Transparent nightdresses made all of lace'
Virgins may squeak
'My dear      I should faint!'
Flutter . . . . . flutter . . . . flutter . . . .
. . . . 'And then      the man—'
Wasting our giggles
For we have no dots

We have been taught
Love is a god

White            with soft wings
                    Nobody shouts
                Virgins for sale
Yet where are our coins
For buying a purchaser

Love is a god
                Marriage expensive
A secret well kept
Makes the noise of the world
Nature's arms spread wide
Making room for us
                Room for all of us
Somebody who was never
                        a virgin
Has bolted the door
Put curtains at our windows

See the men pass
They      are going somewhere

Flesh like weeds
Sprout in the light
So much flesh in the world
                Wanders at will

Spread      behind curtains
Throbs to the night
Bait        to the stars

Spread it with gold
And you carry it home
Against your shirt front
To      a shaded light
With the door locked
Against virgins who
Might      scratch

# Babies In Hospital

## I.

Small Elena
Of shrunken limbs
And ample sex
Who
Having filched
The atrophied
Woman-smile of your mother
Scatter it
On the eating unseen
Tuberculous

Inaudible hands
On the counter-pane
It might have been
Impossible
Fingers should be so long
Being so tiny
But Nature
Needing no microscope
In her laboratory
Found it just as easy
Marshalling imperceptible
Hosts
To bone of your arm
Among overlapping of lint
Attaining a dignity
Unworthy of your years
Two and a half!

## II.

Hail to you
Bad little boy
Lying
In bound beauty
Of only a broken leg
And thank you
For throwing
Your bricks on the floor
For the third time
And the smack
You gave me
For the thermometer

Delightfully male
Already gallant
You smooth the mackintosh
For Elena to sit on beside you
Her fragility
Being irresistibly for you
You are very wise
Precocious coquette
Who never learnt to talk
To look at him
Before
Your semi-imbecile
Eyes shut
It is not given to each of us
To be desired.

### III.

Tend
Do not touch
Apparent flowers
Of festering secret
And the fly-by-nights
Such little things
I cannot be your mother
There are already
So many ignorances
I am not guilty of.

## At The Door
## Of The House

A thousand women's eyes
Riveted to the unrealisable
Scatter the wash-stand of the card-teller
Defiled marble of Carrara
    On which she spreads
Color-picture maps of destiny
In the corner
Of an incondusive bed-room

"Impassioned
Doubly impassioned
Sad
You see these three cards
But here is the double Victory
And there is an elderly lady
Ill    in whom you are concerned
This is the Devil
And these two skeletons
Are mortifications
You    are going to make a journey


At evening    about love
Here is the Man of the Heart
Turning his shoulders to a lady
Covered with tears about matrimony

At the door of your house
There is a letter about an affair
And a bed and a table
And this ace of spades turned upside-down
'With respect'
Means     that some man
Has     well you know
Intentions     little honorable


Here you are     covered with tears
For a deception
The Man of the Heart
Is in thoughtfulness for a letter
He will make a journey at evening
And really     lady
I should say
It will not be long before you see him
For there he is at the door of the house

And look
Here are you
And here is he
In life and thought
At the door of the house"

Muddled among the analine brightness
of the Tauro cards

The wheels with wings
The rows on rows of goblets
　　Passionate magenta blossoms
Hermits　—bring luck—
Moons　　Prison-fortresses
Cudgels
A man cut in half
　　Means a deception
And the nude woman
　　Stands for the world
　　Those eyes

Of Petronilla Lucia Letizia
　　Felicita
Filomena Amalia
Orsola Geltrude Caterina Delfina
Zita Bibiana　　Tarsilla
Eufemia,
Looking for the little love-tale
That never came true
At the door of the house

# Human Cylinders

The human cylinders
Revolving in the enervating dusk
That wraps each closer in the mystery
Of singularity
Among the litter of a sunless afternoon
Having eaten without tasting
Talked without communion
And at least two of us
Loved a very little
Without seeking
To know if our two miseries
In the lucid rush-together of automatons
Could form one opulent well-being

Simplifications of men
In the enervating dusk
Your indistinctness
Serves me the core of the kernel of you
When in the frenzied reaching-out
    of intellect to intellect
Leaning brow to brow    communicative
Over the abyss of the potential
Concordance of respiration
Shames
Absence of corresponding
    between the verbal sensory
And reciprocity
Of conception
And expression

Where each extrudes beyond
    the tangible
One thin pale trail of speculation
From among us we have sent out
Into the enervating dusk
One little whining beast
Whose longing
Is to slink back to antedeluvian burrow
And one elastic tentacle of intuition
To quiver among the stars

The impartiality of the absolute
Routs     the polemic
Or which of us
Would not
Receiving the holy-ghost
Catch it    and caging
    Lose it
Or in the problematic
Destroy the Universe
    With a solution.

# Ignoramus

Shut it up

Sing silence
To destiny
Give    half-a-crown
To a magician
Half a glance
To window-eclipse
And count the glumes
Of your day's bargaining
Lying
In the lining
Of your pocket
               While compromising
Between the perpendicular and horizontal
Some other tramp
Leans against
The night-nursery of trams

Puffs of black night
Quiver the neck
Of the Clown of Fortune
            Dribble out of his trouser-ends
In dust-to-dust
Till    cock-kingdom-come-crow


You can hear the heart-beating
Accoupling
of the masculine and feminine
Universal principles
Mating
And the martyrdom of morning
Caged with the love of houseflies
The avidity of youth
And incommensuration.

Day-spring
Bursting on repetition
      "My friend the Sun
        You have probably met before"
Or breakfasting on rain
You hurry
To interpolate
The over-growth
Of vegetation
With a walking-stick


Or smear a friend
With a greasy residuum
From boiling your soul down
      You can walk to Empyrean
            to-gether
Under the same
Oil-silk umbrella

"I must have you
Count stars for me
Out of their numeral excess
Please keep the brightest
For the last"

# The Dead

We have flowed out of ourselves
Beginning on the outside
That shrivvable skin
Where you leave off

    Of infinite elastic
    Walking the ceiling
    Our eyelashes polish stars

Curled close in the youngest corpuscle
Of a descendant
We spit up our passions in our grand-dams




Fixing the extension of your reactions
Our shadow lengthens
In your fear
You are so old
Born in our immortality
Stuck fast as Life
In one impalpable
Omniprevalent Dimension

We are turned inside out
Your cities lie digesting in our stomachs
Street lights footle in our ocular darkness


Having swallowed your irate hungers
Satisfied before bread-breaking
To your dissolution
We splinter into Wholes
Stirring the remorses of your tomorrow
Among the refuse of your unborn centuries
In our busy ashbins
Stink the melodies
Of your
So easily reducible
Adolescences

Our tissue is of that which escapes you
Birth-Breaths and orgasms
The shattering tremor of the static
The far-shore of an instant
The unsurpassable openness of the circle
Legerdemain of God
Only in the segregated angles
    of Lunatic Asylums
Do those who have strained to
    exceeding themselves
Break on our edgeless contours

The mouthed echoes of what
Has exuded to our companionship
Is horrible to the ear
Of the half that is left inside them.

# O Hell

To clear the drifts of spring
Of our forbears' excrements
And bury the subconscious archives
Under unaffected flowers

Indeed—

Our person is a covered entrance to infinity
Choked with the tatters of tradition

Goddesses and Young Gods
Caress the sanctity of Adolescence
In the shaft to the sun.

# P o e

a lyric elixir of death

    embalms
    the spindle spirits of your hour glass loves
                      on moon spun nights

sets

      icicled canopy
      for corpses of poesy
      with roses and northern lights

    Where frozen nightingales in ilex aisles

                  sing burial rites

# Mexican Desert

The belching ghost-wail of the locomotive
trailing her rattling wooden tail
into the jazz-band sunset. . . .

The mountains in a row
set pinnacles of ferocious isolation
under the alien hot heaven

Vegetable cripples of drought
thrust up the parching appeal
cracking open the earth
stump-fingered cacti
and hunch-back palm trees
belabour the cinders of twilight. . . .

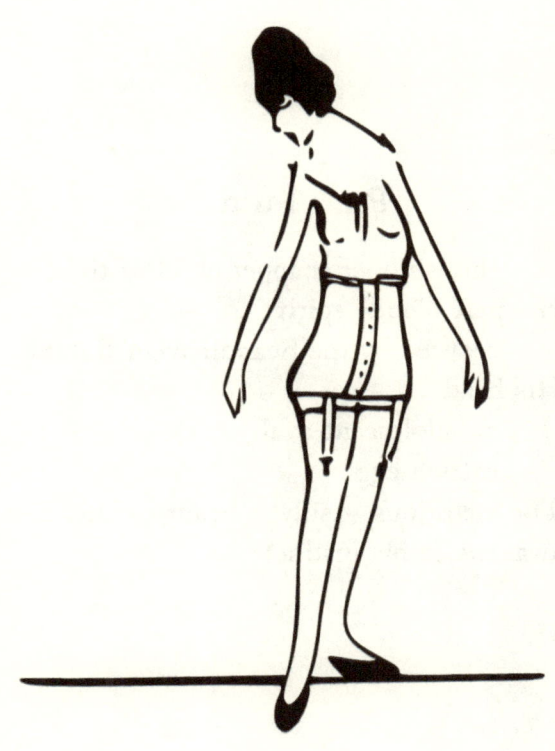

# Perlun

    the whipper snapper child of the sun
His pert blonde spirit
    scoured by the Scandinavian Boreas
His head
    an adolescent oval
    ostrich egg
The victorious    silly    beauty of his face
awakens to his instincts

A vivacious knick-knack tipped with gold
      he puts the world
      to the test of intuition

      Smiling from ear to ear
      Living from other hands to mouth




Holding in immaculate arms
          the syphilitic sailor
          on his avoided death bunk
          or the movie vamp
among the muffled shadows of the shrubberies——

Picking lemons in Los Angeles     broke

The education of "Prince Fils à Papa"
How low men die
How women love—

The rituals of Dempsey and Carpentier

PERLUN
asks "Do these flappers of the millionaires
think i'm a doll for anyone to pat?"

# Brancusi's Golden Bird

The toy
become the aesthetic archetype

As if

some patient peasant God
had rubbed and rubbed
the Alpha and Omega
of Form
into a lump of metal

A naked orientation
unwinged unplumed
        —the ultimate rhythm
has lopped the extremities
of crest and claw
from
the nucleus of flight




The absolute act
of art
conformed
to continent sculpture
—bare as the brow of Osiris—
this breast of revelation

an incandescent curve
licked by chromatic flames
in labyrinths of reflections

This gong
of polished hyperaesthesia
shrills with brass
as the aggressive light
strikes
its significance

The immaculate
conception
of the inaudible bird
occurs
in gorgeous reticence

## "The Starry Sky" Of Wyndham Lewis

who raised
these rocks of human mist

pyramidical survivors
in the cyclorama of space

In the
austere theatre of the Infinite
        the ghosts of the stars
perform the "Presence"

Their celibate shadows
fall
upon the aged radiance
of suns and moons


——The nerves of Heaven
    flinching
    from the antennae
    of the intellect
——the rays
    that pierce
    the nocturnal heart

The airy eyes of angels
the sublime
experiment in pointillism
faded away

The celestial conservatories
blooming with light
are all blown out

Enviable immigrants
into the pure dimension
immune    serene
devourers of the morning stars of Job

Jehovah's seven days
err in your silent entrails
of geometric Chimeras

The Nirvanic snows
drift — — —
to sky worn images

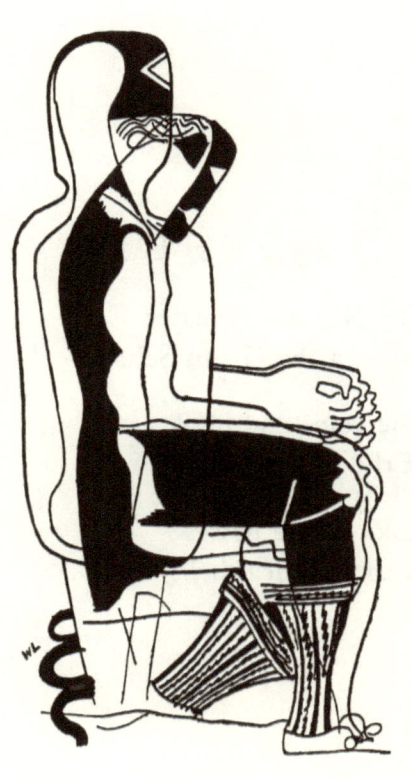

# Joyce's Ulysses

The Normal Monster
sings in the Green Sahara

The voice and offal
of the image of God

make Celtic noises
in these lyrical hells

Hurricanes
of reasoned musics
reap the uncensored earth

The loquent consciousness
of living things
pours in torrential languages

The elderly colloquists
the Spirit and the Flesh
are out of tongue — — —

The Spirit
is impaled upon the phallus

Phoenix
of Irish fires
lighten the Occident

with Ireland's wings
flap pandemoniums
of Olympian prose

and satirize
the imperial Rose
of Gaelic perfumes
—England
the sadistic mother
embraces Erin—

   Master
   of meteoric idiom
   present

The word made flesh
and feeding upon itself
with erudite fangs
The sanguine
introspection of the womb

Don Juan
of Judea
upon a pilgrimage
to the Libido

The Press — — —
purring
its lullabies to sanity

Christ capitalized
scourging
incontrite usurers of destiny
—in hole and corner temples

　And hang
The soul's advertisements
outside the ecclesiast's Zoo

A gravid day
spawns
gutteral gargoyles
upon the Tower of Babel

Empyrean emporium
where the
rejector-recreator
Joyce
flashes the giant reflector
on the sub rosa — — —

# Apology Of Genius

Ostracized as we are with God—
  The watchers of the civilized wastes
  reverse their signals on our track

Lepers of the moon
  all magically diseased
  we come among you
  innocent
  of our luminous sores

. . . . . . . . . . . . . .

We are the sacerdotal clowns
  who feed upon the wind and stars
  and pulverous pastures of poverty

Our wills are formed
  by curious disciplines
  beyond your laws

You may give birth to us
or marry us
the chances of your flesh
are not our destiny—

The cuirass of the soul
still shines—
And we are unaware
if you confuse
such brief
corrosion with possession

In the raw caverns of the Increate
we forge the dusk of Chaos
to that imperious jewelry of the
Universe
—The Beautiful—

While to your eyes
A delicate crop
of criminal mystic immortelles
stands to the censor's scythe

# M a r b l e

Greece has thrown     white shadows
sown
their eyeballs with oblivion

A flock of stone
Gods
perched upon pedestals

A populace
of athlete lilies
of the galleries

scoop the facades of space
with spiral curves
of idol substances
in the silence

A colonnade
Apollo haunts Apollo
with the shade
of a lost hand

# Gertrude Stein

Curie
of the laboratory
of vocabulary
    she crushed
the tonnage
of consciousness
congealed to phrases
    to extract
a radium of the word

# OTHER *Words*

# 1914–1921.

"Free Verse, why I wrote free verse twenty years ago"—?

Yet while Eilshemius exonerates himself from ever having studied the works of any period whatsoever, there is a something Elizabethian about him.

I will end this rummage of a gold-mine with Eilshemius when he is most himself—in the the poems "A Country Child" and "Maggie the Geyser Guide."

"It dwelled, where I would not to live;
In a hut, with cracks and holes.
But there it played with wicker and mud;
And it tried to lift long poles."
"Have you no fear of all those boiling waters?"
"Nay, I was 'hatched' right on this steaming
earth.
The other place cannot be worse!" she ventured,
And in our eyes a twinkle suddenly had birth.
Thus questioning, she grew more sweet to me,
for in her voice
Lay mellow dreaminess, that made my heart
rejoice.

Anyhow, Duchamp meditating the levelling of all values, witnesses the elimination of Sophistication.

MINA LOY.

## In . . . Formation

I do not suppose the Independents "will educate the public"—the only trouble with the public is education.

*The Artist* is uneducated, is seeing IT for the first time; he can never see the same thing twice.

Education is the putting of spectacles on wholesome eyes. The public does not naturally care about these spectacles, the cause of its quarrels with art. *The Public* likes to be jolly; *The Artist* is jolly and quite irresponsible. Art is *The Divine Joke,* and any *Public,* and any *Artist* can see a nice, easy, simple joke, such as the sun; but only artists and serious critics can look at a grayish stickiness on smooth canvas.

Education in recognizing something that has been seen before demands an art that is only acknowledgable by way of diluted comparisons . . . it is significant that the demand is half-hearted.

"Let us forget," is the cry of the educator; "the democratically simple beginnings of an art,"—so that we may talk of those things that have only middle and no end, and together wallow in gray stickiness.

The Public knows better than this, knowing such values as the under-inner curve of women's footgear, one factor of the art of our epoch . . . it is unconcerned with curved Faun's legs and maline twirled scarves of artistic imagining; or with allegories of Life with thorn-skewered eyes . . . it knew before the Futurists that Life is a jolly noise and a rush and sequence cf ample reactions.

*The Artist* then says to *The Public,* "Poor pal; what has happened to you? . . . We were born so similar—and *now* look!" But the Public will not look; that is, look at *The Artist*—it has unnaturally acquired prejudice.

So *The Public* and *The Artist* can meet at every point except the—for *The Artist*—vital one, that of pure uneducated *seeing.* They like the same drinks, can fight in the same trenches, pretend to the same women; but never see the same thing *ONCE.*

You might, at least, keep quiet while I am talking.

MINA LOY.

## APHORISMS ON FUTURISM

DIE in the Past
Live in the Future.

THE velocity of velocities arrives in starting.

IN pressing the material to derive its essence, matter becomes deformed.

AND form hurtling against itself is thrown beyond the synopsis of vision.

THE straight line and the circle are the parents of design, form the basis of art; there is no limit to their coherent variability.

LOVE the hideous in order to find the sublime core of it.

OPEN your arms to the delapidated, to rehabilitate them.

YOU prefer to observe the past on which your eyes are already opened.

BUT the Future is only dark from outside.
*Leap* into it—and it EXPLODES with *Light*.

FORGET that you live in houses, that you may live in yourself—

FOR the smallest people live in the greatest houses.

BUT the smallest person, potentially, is as great as the Universe.

WHAT can you know of expansion, who limit yourselves to compromise?

HITHERTO the great man has achieved greatness by keeping the people small.

BUT in the Future, by inspiring the people to expand to their fullest capacity, the great man proportionately must be tremendous—a God.

LOVE of others is the appreciation of one's self.

MAY your egotism be so gigantic that you comprise mankind in your self-sympathy.

THE Future is limitless—the past a trail of insidious reactions.

LIFE is only limited by our prejudices. Destroy them, and you cease to be at the mercy of yourself.

TIME is the dispersion of intensiveness.

THE Futurist can live a thousand years in one poem.

HE can compress every æsthetic principle in one line.

THE mind is a magician bound by assimilations; let him loose and the smallest idea conceived in freedom will suffice to negate the wisdom of all forefathers.

LOOKING on the past you arrive at "Yes," but before you can act upon it you have already arrived at "NO."

THE Futurist must leap from affirmative to affirmative, ignoring intermittent negations—must spring from stepping-stone to stone of creative exploration; without slipping back into the turbid stream of accepted facts.

THERE are no excrescences on the absolute, to which man may pin his faith.

TODAY is the crisis in consciousness.

CONSCIOUSNESS cannot spontaneously accept or reject new forms, as offered by creative genius; it is the new form, for however great a period of time it may remain a mere irritant—that moulds consciousness to the necessary amplitude for holding it.

CONSCIOUSNESS has no climax.

LET the Universe flow into your consciousness, there is no limit to its capacity, nothing that it shall not re-create.

UNSCREW your capability of absorption and grasp the elements of Life
—*Whole*.

MISERY is in the disintegration of Joy;
Intellect, of Intuition;
Acceptance, of Inspiration.

CEASE to build up your personality with the ejections of irrelevant minds.

NOT to be a cipher in your ambient,
But to color your ambient with your preferences.

NOT to accept experience at its face value.

BUT to readjust activity to the peculiarity of your own will.

THESE are the primary tentatives towards independence.

MAN is a slave only to his own mental lethargy.

YOU cannot restrict the mind's capacity.

THEREFORE you stand not only in abject servitude to your perceptive consciousness—

BUT also to the mechanical re-actions of the subconsciousness, that rubbish heap of tradition—

AND believing yourself free—your least conception is colored by the pigment of retrograde superstitions.

HERE are the fallow-lands of mental spatiality that Futurism will clear—

MAKING place for whatever you are brave enough, beautiful enough to draw out of the realized self.

TO your blushing we shout the obscenities, we scream the blasphemies, that you, being weak, whisper alone in the dark.

THEY are empty except of your shame.

AND so these sounds shall dissolve back to their innate senselessness.

THUS shall evolve the language of the Future.

THROUGH derision of Humanity as it appears—

TO arrive at respect for man as he shall be—

ACCEPT the tremendous truth of Futurism
Leaving all those
      —Knick-knacks.—

MINA LOY.

# PSYCHO-DEMOCRACY

## a movement to focus human reason

### on

## THE CONSCIOUS DIRECTION OF EVOLUTION

to replace the cataclysmic factor in social evolution WAR. An absolute, constructive and liberating ideal put to the will of mankind for acceptance or rejection.

*Psycho democracy is*

Democracy of The Spirit, government by creative imagination, participation in essential wisdom—Fraternity of Intuition, the Intellect and Mother wit. (The Creator, the scholar, the natural man).

A psychological gauge applied to all social problems, for the interpretation of political, religious and financial systems.

Democratic interchange and valuation of *ideas.*

The Substitution of consciously directed evolution for revolution, *Creative inspiration for Force,* Laughter for Lethargy, Sociability for Sociology, Human psychology for Tradition.

The Psycho-Democratic Policy is
Habeas Animum.

"To illuminate the earth with her peoples eyes."

*The organization of Psycho-Democracy* is based on the laws of psychic evolution, our principles spring from Intuition, and are presented to man's intellect for maturation.

We make the experiment of a "collectivity" moved by the same intellectual logic as are the tactics of the successful individual reckoning with "actual" values and following the rules of the game of life, influencing our era by right of the merits of our (collective) personality.

Most movements have a fixed concept towards which they advance, we move away from all fixed concepts in order to advance.


### The Psycho-democrat is

Man, Woman or Child of good sense and with imagination, having a normal love of Life and a sympathic indifference to their neighbours obligations.

The *living* successor of that travesty of man; the *Dummy Public* originated by the Press, financed by the Capitalist:

For whom the politician legislates,
The army fights,
The church collects.

THE IDEA-FABRIC OF HUMAN SOCIETY. Modern social existence is a form of psychic activity based on *Ideas* promoted by the self-conscious minority of *Power.*

Every phase in evolution has been marked by the different kinds of ideas for which men tortured one another.

Society today is composed of distinctly different human strata; heirs of the different ideas for which men tortured one another.

The Tediousness of Human Evolution is owing:

To the tendency of ideas to outlast their origin, i. e. the tendency of human institutions to outlast the psychological conditions from which they arose.

Psycho-Democracy considers social institutions as structural forms in collective consciousness which are subject to the same evolutional transformation as is collective consciousness itself, and that our social institutions of today will cause future generations to roar with laughter.

### Criminal Lunacy

In the very near future the fact that it is considered either normal or necessary for millions of men and women to wear out their organisms with no reward but the maintainance of those organisms, imperfectly functioning, and that this social condition should be safeguarded and preserved by the blowing up of other millions of human organisms will appear as the nightmare of a criminal lunatic.

### Cosmic Neurosis

The destructive element in collective consciousness induced by inhibitive social and religious precepts that ordain that man must suffer and cause to suffer and deny the validity of Man's fundamental desires, has resulted in Cosmic Neurosis, whose major symptom is Fear.

This fear takes the form of international suspicion and the resulting national protective-phobias.

Our enlightened psychological principles will put an end to Cosmic Neurosis.

### Psychic Evolution

This thing called *Life* which seems to be the impact of luminous bodies, knocking sparks off one another in chaos, will be transformed through Psycho-Democratic evolution from a war between good and evil, i. e. (between beneficent and painful chance) to a competition between different kinds of good: (beneficent spontaneities),

*The Paradox of the Dominator and the Dominated.*

"Class" is a psychological condition.

The one class distinction is between the dominator and the dominated.

Every social upheaval has been the evolutional phenomenon of the recruiting of new material to the dominating class. A class victory is never the promotion of one class to the status of another class, but the shifting of certain elements in the victorious class to the psychological condition of the dominating class.

The dominating class is a psychological nucleus progressively absorbing all similar elements into itself. It is therefore our important task to elucidate the psychology of the Dominator, for the dominated, as the Basis of intrinsic democracy.

*Power* is a secret society of the minority, whose hold on the majority lies in the esoteric or actual value of social ideas.

This esoteric value is unrevealed to the majority, being:—

1) The transmutability of the *strategical ideas* of the minority into *social ideals* for the majority.

2) The value of *social ideals* as a means of conserving the majority as a plastic psychic material with which *Power* moulds the contours of its own supremacy.

3) The value of the exoteric or public representation of social ideals as limiting the unit for the advantage of a collectivity, while in reality insuring the advantage of the minority with the consent of the majority.

The ensuing confusion in the public mind between its innate logic and the social ideals dictated by the Dominator, provides the *Paradox of the Dominator and the Dominated;* for it is at once the vantage ground for the Dominator's tactics and the blind force which at recurrent intervals confounds the self-conscious minority of *Power.*

### Psycho-Democratic Aesthetic

The æthetic contour of a people is formed by its habits.

Man's evolution through his circumstances has resulted in his point of view.

His point of view forms his habits.

The Dominator's standard has been the most highly evolved human habit. Therefore class evolution must democratize the Dominator's standard, which hitherto evolved by circumstances, will in future spring directly into "habit" out of a "point of view."

### *The Aim of Society is the Perfection of Self*

Man's desire is for Self.

His desire is commensurate with possibility.

The earth offers super-abundance for All.

Human imagination is illimitable.

Psycho-Democracy advocates the fulfilment of all Desire.

"Self" is the covered entrance to Infinity.

### *Militarism*

Militarism forms the nucleus of national *Influential symbolism;* the flag, the uniform; inspires the *Rhythm of national popular enthusiasm:* the march, the band, parade. Sustains the *belligerent masculine* social ideal. Like all concentrated human forces it is *psychically magnetic.*

It has created certain formulæ figuring largely in our social pleasures, which no other social institution affords; the inevitable "snobbery" thus involved insures its protracted success.

### *Pacifism*

The sole opposition to this imposing and efficiently organized social foundation is the pacifist *Dont.*

Pacifism has not yet offered a creative substitute for the military ideal, but a negative conception which leaves a void in social psychological construction, without providing any adequate suggestions as to how this void should be filled.

*The Appeal of psycho-Democracy* for the conscious direction of evolution, is an appeal to the thinker, the scientist, the philosopher, the writer, the artist, the mechanic, the worker, to join intelligent forces in a concerted effort to evolve and establish *a new social symbolism, a new social rhythm, a new social snobism* with a human psychological significance of equal value to that of militarism.

To consider that the belligerent tendency in human nature which is at present abnormaly fostered by social institutions and education, can be superseded by another of the different tendencies in human nature, if developed through transformed social institutions and revised education.

*To vindicate Humanity's claim to a Divine Destiny.* Not to endeavor to eliminate the indestructable forces in human nature but to establish a new social system for their utilization. To present intellectual heroism as a popular ideal in place of physical heroism encouraging the expression of individual psychology in place of mob-psychology. To believe that man has the conceptual power to create a substitute for war, having the same stimulus to action as the hazard of death, the same spur to renassence as devastation, and that his mentality will evolve new forms of expressive action to inspire him to such ebullitions of enthusiasm as does the call to arms.

In *Psycho-Democracy* shall arise men and women whose strength and originality of conception will concrete a vital ideal as the basis of International politics. This ideal which is in a nebulous state, once defined will be easier to impose on humanity than the hypnotic war lust.

For it is but logical to suppose that if the slight amount of magnetism in the make up of the world's leaders of today, is sufficient to rush great peoples on to death and agony, it will be a simple task to persuade great peoples to the effort of self realization in a life amplifying ideal; and to apply the force of reason to the solution of their life problems, which have been so acutely aggravated by the force of explosives.

And to dissuade Man from any longer considering his destiny as being extraneous to his logic.

MINA LOY.

*Buenos Aires, 1918.*

**Who's Who in** *by Clara*

Aileen Dresser, Painter

Mary Myers, Designer of Pavlowa
Costumes

Beatrix Sherman, Silhouettist

Mina Loy, Painter-Poet

Lou Arensberg

Louise Norton,
Writer

Frances Stevens, Futurist
Painter and Horsewoman

# Manhattan
## Tice

Beulah Livingstone, Press Agent

Betty Turner, Actress

Helena Smith-Dayton, Sculptress

Daisy Thompson, Shop of
Beautiful Things

Ethel Plummer, Artist

Fania Mar noff, Actress

*This Space for Your*
*Thoughts*

THE OLD EXPRESSIONS ARE WITH US ALWAYS
AND THERE ARE ALWAYS OTHERS

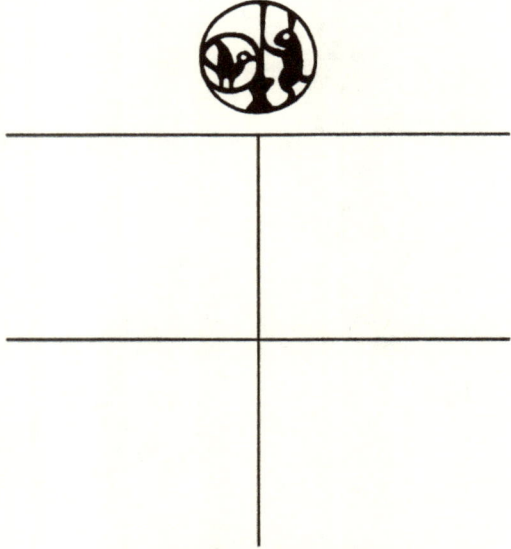

Please handle with care.

www.ingramcontent.com/pod-product-compliance
Lightning Source LLC
Chambersburg PA
CBHW031419120626
46545CB00006B/2185